Table of C

Company's Coming Cookbooks

COMPANY'S COMING SERIES

- 150 Delicious Squares
- Casseroles
- Muffins & More
- Salads
- Appetizers
- Desserts
- Soups & Sandwiches
- Holiday Entertaining
- Cookies
- Vegetables
- Main Courses
- Pasta
- Cakes
- Barbecues
- Dinners of the World
- Lunches
- Pies
- Light Recipes
- Microwave Cooking
- Preserves
- Light Casseroles
- Chicken, Etc.
- Kids Cooking
- Fish & Seafood
- Breads
- Meatless Cooking
- Cooking for Two
- Breakfasts & Brunches
- Slow Cooker Recipes
- Pizza!
- One-Dish Meals
- Starters (November 1999)

SELECT SERIES

- Sauces & Marinades
- Ground Beef
- Beans & Rice
- 30-Minute Meals
- Make-Ahead Salads
- No-Bake Desserts

GREATEST HITS

- Biscuits, Muffins & Loaves
- Dips, Spreads & Dressings

KIDS COOKBOOKS

- Kids - Lunches
- Kids - Snacks

LOW-FAT SERIES

- Low-Fat Cooking
- Low-Fat Pasta

OTHER TITLES

- Company's Coming for Christmas
- Easy Entertaining
- Millennium Edition (September 1999)

Foreword

No matter how many years I've been cooking and catering, I'm still amazed at the new tips and tricks I learn; either through asking others, through trial and error, through reading and testing, and often times, I learn from you—the readers! In any case, these lessons come through necessity. Usually, something goes wrong—a recipe fails, a cake falls, or a jellied salad doesn't set. **Cooking Tips** will help you through these cooking calamities.

In this book, we offer you baking tips, tips on cooking with eggs, helpful hints about fish, and much more. Sometimes, the household chef just needs a little more knowledge to come up with a simple solution. **Cooking Tips** provides that for you. It includes shortcuts, substitutions, and descriptions of ingredients you tend to stay away from, simply because you may not know enough about them yet. What do you really know about the various types of beans, spices, and vinegars? We've added helpful hints on how to use these lesser known ingredients.

We know our readers have great tips too, so we've provided some space for you to jot down your own successes and cooking solutions. If you've discovered other tips that work for you write them down in the space provided. Throughout the years, I've learned there is often more than one solution to a cooking dilemma. And you've likely discovered your own shortcuts and substitutes; so there's room for you to make notes at the end of those sections.

Whether you've run into a problem, run out of a special ingredient, run out of time, or just want to run—**Cooking Tips** will provide you with some invaluable answers to get you back on track!

Jean Paré

The Jean Paré Story

Jean Paré grew up understanding that the combination of family, friends and home cooking is the essence of a good life. From her mother she learned to appreciate good cooking, while her father praised even her earliest attempts. When she left home she took with her many acquired family recipes, her love of cooking and her intriguing desire to read recipe books like novels!

In 1963, when her four children had all reached school age, Jean volunteered to cater to the 50th anniversary of the Vermilion School of Agriculture, now Lakeland College. Working out of her home, Jean prepared a dinner for over 1000 people which launched a flourishing catering operation that continued for over eighteen years. During that time she was provided with countless opportunities to test new ideas with immediate feedback—resulting in empty plates and contented customers! Whether preparing cocktail sandwiches for a house party or serving a hot meal for 1500 people, Jean Paré earned a reputation for good food, courteous service and reasonable prices.

"Why don't you write a cookbook?" Time and again, as requests for her recipes mounted, Jean was asked that question. Jean's response was to team up with her son, Grant Lovig, in the fall of 1980 to form Company's Coming Publishing Limited. April 14, 1981, marked the debut of "150 DELICIOUS SQUARES", the first Company's Coming cookbook in what soon would become Canada's most popular cookbook series.

Jean Paré's operation has grown steadily from the early days of working out of a spare bedroom in her home. Full-time staff includes marketing personnel located in major cities across Canada. Home Office is based in Edmonton, Alberta in a modern building constructed specially for the company.

Today the company distributes throughout Canada and the United States in addition to numerous overseas markets, all under the guidance of Jean's daughter, Gail Lovig. Best-sellers many times over, Company's Coming cookbooks are published in English and French, plus a Spanish-language edition is available in Mexico. Familiar and trusted in home kitchens the world over, Company's Coming cookbooks are offered in a variety of formats, including the original softcover series.

Jean Paré's approach to cooking has always called for quick and easy recipes using everyday ingredients. Even when travelling, she is constantly on the lookout for new ideas to share with her readers. At home, she can usually be found researching and writing recipes, or working in the company's test kitchen. Jean continues to gain new supporters by adhering to what she calls "the golden rule of cooking": never share a recipe you wouldn't use yourself. It's an approach that works—*millions of times over!*

Baking Tips

Cakes

▶ If your cake has fallen in the center:

• the wet ingredients (margarine, sugar, eggs) may have been underbeaten or the batter may have been overbeaten after adding the dry ingredients.

• there may be too much sugar, baking powder or liquid, or not enough flour.

• you may have opened the oven door before your cake has set or closed the oven door too hard.

▶ If your cake has peaked in the center:

• the oven most likely was too hot, causing the cake to rise too quickly.

• it could be caused by overbeating after the flour was added, which overactivates the gluten in the flour, creating a tough cake.

▶ When making a pound cake, remember to beat in each egg well before adding the next one and don't use too high a speed on the mixer.

▶ Almost all commercial flours have been presifted. It is, however, a good idea to sift your flour if you are making a delicate cake that has little or no chemical leavening, such as angel food, sponge and pound cake. It provides the extra aeration these cakes require.

▶ When combining 2 single layer cakes to make a double layer cake, turn the cake that will be on the bottom, upside down. This way, your middle filling will be between 2 flat sides. The rounded top side of the second cake makes the nicer top for the overall cake.

Frostings & Icings

▶ When frosting a single layer cake does it matter whether you use the top side or the bottom side? No, it's a personal preference, but typically the rounded top side is used.

▶ The terms frosting and icing are often used interchangeably. Frostings are generally thicker than icings and can be swirled and textured more easily. Icings are thinner but still hold their shape.

▶ Glaze has more liquid than either frosting or icing; it is either poured or brushed over a cake or pastry. A glaze can be a mixture of sugar and a liquid (such as milk, water, melted jelly or juice) depending on the flavor and color you are looking for. Glazes are generally paired with cakes and pastries that have a strong flavor of their own, such as chiffon cakes, fruit tarts and sweet rolls.

Cheesecakes

▶ Cracks in cheesecakes are such a common complaint from cooks. Several things might be the cause:

• Usually the temp-erature of the oven is too high, which causes the outside of the cake to set before the inside has had time to expand and settle; cheese-cakes should bake slowly. The best temperature is 325 to 350°F (160 to 175°C).

• Overbeating cheesecake batter can cause cracks. When too much air is incorporated into the mixture, it will rise and then collapse and split. Beat in the eggs, 1 at a time, on low until just blended.

▶ As soon as you remove your cheesecake from the oven, place it on a wire cooling rack and run a knife around the edge of the pan. This way, as the center settles, so will the outer edge, keeping the top nice and flat.

▶ If cracks do appear in your next cheesecake, despite all precautions, fill them with whipped topping and ignore them. The cake will taste just as wonderful and be eaten just as fast with or without cracks!

Baking Tips

General

▶ To measure liquid ingredients, use clear glass or plastic measuring cups with spouts. Always place container on a level surface, then pour in what you need, viewing from the side at eye level to fill to the correct level.

▶ To measure dry or solid ingredients (such as flour or yogurt), use plastic or metal dry measuring cups. Their flat tops allow you to fill the cup to the top and then level off the ingredients with a knife or straight edge.

▶ When dry ingredients, such as baking powder, salt and spices are to be added to flour, first measure them into a small cup. So often, we forget if we added 1 or 2 tsp. (5 or 10 mL), or we get interrupted. This way, the rest of the dry ingredients (such as flour or sugar), won't be at risk if you have to start over.

▶ Baking powder should be stirred before using as it does settle.

▶ If your baking powder doesn't have an expiry date on it, write the date on the bottom of the can; it can be a year old very quickly. To test if you should discard your old baking powder, measure ¼ cup (60 mL) hot tap water. Stir in ½ tsp. (2 mL) baking powder. It should bubble actively.

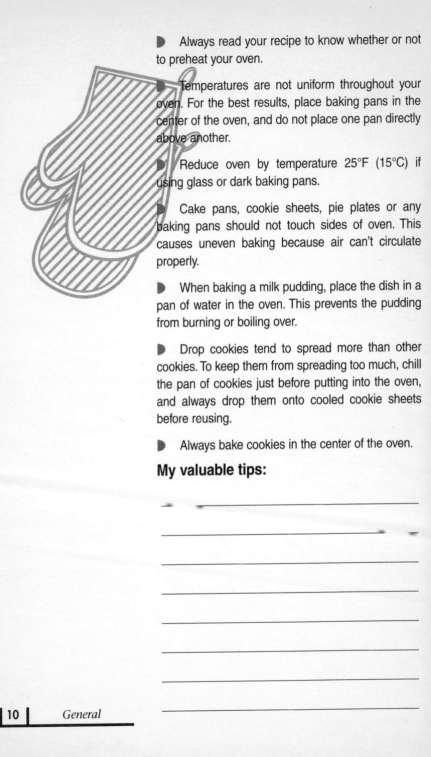

▶ Always read your recipe to know whether or not to preheat your oven.

▶ Temperatures are not uniform throughout your oven. For the best results, place baking pans in the center of the oven, and do not place one pan directly above another.

▶ Reduce oven by temperature 25°F (15°C) if using glass or dark baking pans.

▶ Cake pans, cookie sheets, pie plates or any baking pans should not touch sides of oven. This causes uneven baking because air can't circulate properly.

▶ When baking a milk pudding, place the dish in a pan of water in the oven. This prevents the pudding from burning or boiling over.

▶ Drop cookies tend to spread more than other cookies. To keep them from spreading too much, chill the pan of cookies just before putting into the oven, and always drop them onto cooled cookie sheets before reusing.

▶ Always bake cookies in the center of the oven.

My valuable tips:

_____

_____

_____

_____

_____

_____

_____

Baking Tips

Pastry & Pies

▶ When making fruit pies keep in mind that fruits vary in sweetness, as does your taste preference for how sweet you like fruit pies. Add less sugar to fruits that are already naturally sweet. If they are very juicy, the sugar will draw out more juice and will make the filling runny.

▶ Common thickeners for fruit pie fillings are flour, cornstarch and tapioca. Flour gives a more opaque appearance to the filling, while cornstarch and tapioca create fillings that are more translucent. If the fruits are too acidic for flour to thicken sufficiently, use one of the other thickeners.

▶ To help with cleanup of those messy spills in your oven when baking pies, set a baking sheet or pizza pan on the shelf below. Immerse baking sheet or pan into hot soapy water as soon as baking is done. Better yet, use a disposable foil oven liner.

▶ When making a pie topped with meringue, always spread the meringue so that it extends to, and touches, the crust. This will prevent it from pulling away from the edge during baking.

▶ For a nice touch on a double crust pie, brush the unbaked top with milk, water or melted margarine or butter, then sprinkle with sugar. Or you can just sprinkle with sugar.

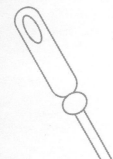

▶ Baking is a precise science and so accurate measurements are critical for best results. Too much flour makes pastry tough; too much shortening makes pastry greasy and crumbly; too much water makes pastry tough and soggy.

For a baked pastry or crumb crust, select a glass pie plate or dull metal pie pan; shiny metal pans will keep crusts from browning properly. Only use shiny metal pans for crumb crusts that are not baked.

To bake an unfilled pie shell, there are two methods that work well. You can either fit the rolled pastry inside the pie pan as usual, or over the outside of an upside down pie pan. Either way, prick the pastry all over with a fork and then place a second pie pan either inside or over top. Neither way will produce a fluted edge – but at least you will have sides! Most unfilled pie shells are baked in a 400°F (205°C) oven for 10 to 15 minutes.

After baking, cool pie on wire rack. This allows air to circulate under the pie and keeps crust from going soggy.

Do you have a few pastry scraps leftover? Sprinkle with cinnamon and sugar and bake like cookies.

My valuable tips:

_____

_____

_____

_____

_____

_____

_____

_____

Baking Tips

Quick Breads

▶ Next time you bake sweet muffins or breads, grease and sugar pans instead of greasing and flouring. It adds a nice touch of sweetness.

▶ Don't overmix muffins or they will be tough. Mix wet ingredients well, then add combined dry ingredients and stir just to moisten.

▶ Use an ice-cream scoop to measure equal amounts of batter for muffins or cookies. Use the smallest size scoop for appetizer meatballs. The scoops are generally available through restaurant supply outlets or kitchen specialty shops.

▶ Fill cake and muffin pans ⅔ to ¾ full. During baking, the batter will rise just to, or slightly above, the rim.

▶ Add a few drops of water to any empty muffin cups in the pan to keep them from burning and to help the muffin pan heat more evenly.

▶ For easier removal, let muffins "rest" in pans for a few minutes after baking.

▶ When mixing biscuit dough be gentle and work quickly, or the biscuits will be tough. Kneading distributes the leaven and develops the gluten in the flour just enough to help the biscuits rise; generally 8 to 10 times is sufficient. With experience you will sense when the dough is ready.

▶ Nut breads (tea loaves) are best stored overnight before cutting. The flavors mellow and the loaves are easier to slice.

▶ When baking nut breads (tea loaves), check the bread 10 to 15 minutes before the baking is complete. Cover with foil if it's browning too fast.

▶ Don't be concerned if your nut bread (tea loaf) has a crack down the top of the loaf. This is typical of these quick breads.

▶ It is so easy to overbake brownies. When the edges start to show signs of pulling slightly away from pan, then test the center with a wooden pick. If it comes out clean but moist, the brownies are done.

My valuable tips:

_____

_____

_____

_____

_____

_____

_____

_____

_____

Baking Tips

Yeast Breads

▶ Yeast requires warm, moist conditions to multiply. Excessive heat above 140°F (60°C) will kill it; excessive cold below 90°F (35°C) will slow it down and reduce its leavening capability. Salt also hampers yeast growth so it is added later with remaining ingredients. Sugar provides food for yeast, helping to speed its growth (although excessive sugar can do just the reverse). Many recipes call for adding sugar to the liquid used for activating the yeast.

▶ Pick a warm, draft-free spot to let dough rise. If you cover the dough with plastic wrap, spray one side of the wrap with no-stick cooking spray first. Or a damp tea towel works well.

▶ A good consistent place to let dough rise is in your oven with the oven light on and the door closed.

▶ When baking several long, individual or round loaves of bread, you'll need an extra large 11 x 17 inch (28 x 43 cm) baking sheet. If you don't have this size baking sheet, shape the loaves on 2 smaller baking sheets and let them rise as directed. Then, while you're baking 1 loaf, place the other one in the refrigerator. Don't have the 2 smaller baking sheets in the oven at the same time; not enough air can circulate in the oven to bake both loaves evenly.

▶ To test whether dough has risen sufficiently, poke 2 fingers into the dough. If it pops back up right away, the dough is ready.

Cooking Tips

Beans

▶ To soak dried beans before cooking, first pick through them to remove any debris. Cover with water and let soak for at least 8 hours or overnight. Follow directions on package if given.

▶ A quicker method for soaking beans is to boil them for 2 minutes, then cover and let stand for 1 hour.

▶ To cook dried beans that have not been presoaked, add 30 minutes to the cooking time.

▶ To cook most dried beans, add the beans to rapidly boiling, salted water. Cover, reduce heat and cook until tender or according to recipe.

▶ If you are short of time, use dried split peas rather than dried whole peas. Split peas do not need to be presoaked before cooking.

▶ Types of Beans:

• Black beans (turtle beans) are pea-sized, jet black oval beans that have an earthy flavor and a soft, mealy texture. They can be bought dried or canned. They are used in such dishes as black beans and rice, black bean soup and black bean sauce.

• Black-eyed peas (black-eyed beans or cowpeas) are cream-colored with a single black spot on their skin. These round legumes have a pea-like flavor and firm texture if not overcooked. They can be bought dried or canned and are often used in casseroles with a combination of other beans.

• Chick peas (garbanzo beans or ceci) are tan-colored and roughly the size and shape of small hazelnuts or acorns. Chick peas have a nut-like flavor and a very firm texture. They can be bought dried or canned and are often used in pasta sauces, in salads, or mashed for hummus or burgers.

• Great Northern beans (haricot beans) are kidney-shaped and are the largest of the white beans. They can be bought dried or canned. Their mild flavor makes them ideal for baked bean recipes, casseroles, soups or stews.

• Kidney beans are named for their shape. These large, meaty beans may be light red, dark red or white. Kidney beans can be bought dried or canned, however, the canned are the most popular. They are especially good in chili but can also be used for soups and casseroles when combined with other beans.

• Lentils are tiny, disk-shaped legumes that come in many colors. The most common are red, brown and green. They cook quickly, need no presoaking and have a distinctive somewhat peppery flavor. They can be used in soups, cooked with other vegetables or served cold in salads. Brown and green lentils hold their shapes well after cooking and are great for salads. Red lentils cook more quickly and work best in purées.

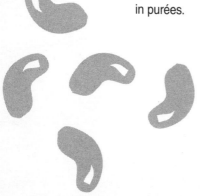

• Lima beans are one of the most widely available beans. They come in 2 sizes. Large limas are called Fordhooks or butter beans. Baby limas (calicos) are a smaller, milder-tasting variety. Both are sold frozen as well as dried and canned. They can be added to soups or served as a vegetable.

• Mung beans are most commonly used for what most of us refer to as bean sprouts. The beans are small greenish-brown, yellow or black legumes with a thicker whitish sprout. Mung beans cook more quickly than most dried beans and become soft and sweet tasting. The sprouts can be bought canned or fresh.

• Navy beans (white peas/beans) are a smaller version of Great Northern beans. These are denser, less mealy and more mildly flavored. They can be bought dried or canned.

• Pinto beans are a medium-sized long "painted" bean, reddish tan and mottled with brown flecks. They can be bought dried or canned and are used frequently in Mexican dishes and can be substituted for kidney beans in chili.

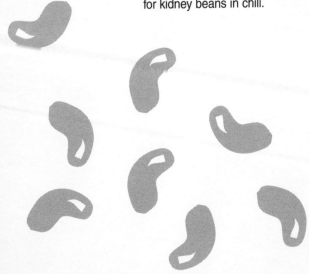

Cooking Tips

Eggs & Cheese

▶ Never add raw egg to a hot liquid (except for Egg Drop Soup!). Always stir a little of the hot liquid into the egg to raise its temperature, beating well. Then whisk warmed egg mixture into remaining hot liquid.

▶ A liquid, such as a soup or sauce, should never be allowed to boil after eggs have been added or it is apt to curdle. The liquid must be heated enough, however, to allow the egg protein to thicken it.

▶ After adding eggs to a base that contains flour, the mixture should be brought to a boil then immediately removed from the heat.

▶ Eggs have a "best before" date on all cartons. Refrigerate eggs promptly after purchasing. When you get down to the last few eggs and want to purchase more, use a felt pen to mark an "x" on the old eggs so they will be used first.

▶ Always serve hot egg dishes right away. Refrigerate chilled egg dishes immediately after mixing, and keep them cold until serving time. Promptly chill leftover or make-ahead dishes containing eggs.

▶ Always discard any eggs with broken or cracked shells. If the shell cracks or breaks as you are putting the eggs away (or because you banged the carton), then the egg will be ok, but should be used immediately. They may have become contaminated with harmful bacteria called salmonella. Hairline markings just on the outside of the shell should be OK.

▶ It's best to use large eggs for baking. Extra large eggs may cause cakes to fall when cooled.

▶ It is easiest to separate eggs when they are cold. Also the yolks are less likely to break.

▶ Egg whites will not beat properly if there is a trace of yolk in them, so it is important to separate eggs carefully. If you have a number of eggs to separate, it's less frustrating if you break each egg separately over a small bowl so as not to get any yolk in your big bowl of egg whites.

▶ If you do get a bit of yolk in your egg whites, touch the yolk with a damp cloth or paper towel. It will pick the yolk up quickly and cleanly.

▶ Eggs beat up fluffier when not too cold. Egg whites, in particular, should be at room temperature for best results.

▶ Beat egg whites with grease-free beaters in a grease-free bowl. Do not use a plastic bowl.

Hard-Boiled Eggs

▶ When hard-boiling eggs, add 1 tsp. (5 mL) vinegar to water to prevent cracking.

▶ To make a perfect hard-boiled egg, poke wider end of egg with egg piercer. Put eggs into cold water. Bring the water to a boil then lower heat to medium. Boil for exactly 10 minutes. Cool in running cold water until no heat can be felt when egg is held for 10 seconds. Refrigerate immediately.

▶ When slicing hard-boiled eggs, wet the knife before cutting to keep the yolk from crumbling. Or purchase an egg slicer that has the thin wire cutters.

▶ Well-chilled hard-boiled eggs peel more easily than room temperature eggs. Gently tap the eggshell on the counter along the egg's equator. To peel, hold egg under running water or peel while immersed in water.

▶ To determine whether an egg is hard-boiled, spin it. If it spins round and round, it is hard-boiled. If it wobbles and will not spin, it is raw.

▶ To color eggs, use cooled hard-boiled eggs. Pour 1 cup (250 mL) hot water and 1 tbsp. (15 mL) white vinegar into a large mug or small ceramic or glass bowl. Add drops of food coloring to create desired color. Add egg. For more intense colors leave egg in the dye longer. Let dry on wire cooling rack with paper towel placed underneath to prevent discoloring counter.

Cheese

▶ For perfect pancakes, always preheat your griddle or skillet over medium-high before pouring on the batter. Test for readiness by sprinkling a few drops of water on the hot surface. If the water jumps, dances or sizzles, the griddle is ready.

▶ Bring cheese to room temperature before melting over low. This helps prevent toughening and separation of oils and liquid.

▶ If your cheese is getting old, grate and place in sealable plastic bag. Freeze. Use in casseroles.

▶ When cutting hard cheese, always hold by the wrapping, exposing only the part to be cut. The salt and oils from your skin will promote spoilage faster if you hold the cheese directly. Cheese holders are also available. They have 3 or 4 prongs that you push into the cheese, leaving a 'handle' to hold.

My valuable tips:

_____

_____

_____

_____

_____

_____

_____

_____

_____

Cooking Tips

Fish & Seafood

▶ Fish should always be thawed in the refrigerator as it is very perishable.

▶ Cooking Fish:

• To bake: Measure thickest part of the fish and allow 10 minutes of cooking time per inch (2.5 cm). Bake in a preheated 450°F (230°C) oven. If fish is wrapped in foil, allow an extra 5 to 8 minutes per inch (2.5 cm) of thickness.

• To fry or grill: They can be fried in butter or hard margarine, or dipped into flour, beaten egg and fried; or fish can be dipped into beaten egg, then bread crumbs and fried. Allow 10 minutes per inch (2.5 cm) of thickness. Sprinkle with salt and pepper or seasoned bread crumbs.

• To poach: Cover fish with water, milk or a Court Bouillon in saucepan. (A Court Bouillon is a liquid consisting of water and either wine, lemon juice or vinegar, seasoned with herbs and spices.) Cover saucepan. Simmer gently for about 5 minutes until fish flakes easily with fork.

▶ Poached or deep-fried fish will cook faster than oven baked fish. Do not overcook fish; it retains heat after being removed from the oven and so will continue to cook a bit more.

▶ If you like fish but don't want everyone else to know that you had it for dinner, here's a little tip. Before cooking the fish, rub it with lemon juice then rinse under cold running water. The acid in the lemon juice will change the nitrogen compounds that give fish its distinctive aroma. After you have handled the fish wash your hands with a little lemon juice. Rinse well.

▶ After cooking fish, wash the pan with vinegar to remove the fishy odor.

▶ To check fish for doneness, insert knife point into the thickest part of the fish's flesh. Properly cooked fish will be opaque and will not cling to the bones.

My valuable tips:

_____

_____

_____

_____

_____

_____

_____

_____

_____

_____

_____

_____

_____

Cooking Tips

Flavor Enhancers

▶ Add onion flakes to enhance the flavor of canned soups.

▶ Add curry powder to enhance the flavor of creamed soups.

▶ Add dill weed to tomato or chicken soup.

▶ A pinch – between thumb and forefinger
A dash – 1 shake
A sprinkle – several "dashes" (shakes)

▶ Using Spices & Herbs:

Allspice: pot roasts, soups, stews, hams, vegetables, baked foods.

Basil: meats, poultry, fish, soups, stews, pasta, stuffings, vegetables, salads, dressings, eggs, dips, sauces.

Bay leaf: corned beef, soups, stews, pot roasts, fish, eggs, dried bean dishes, potatoes, rice, salads, gravies, marinades.

Caraway seed: meatloaves, pot roasts, soups, stews, eggs, stuffings, vegetables, salads, sauerkraut, breads, dips, sauces, spreads.

Cardamom: meats, poultry, fish, fruit, salads, dressings, pastries, breads, cookies, cakes.

Celery (seed, flakes and salt): meats, poultry, soups, stews, eggs, salads, sauces, breads, stuffings, spreads, relishes.

Chili powder: meats, poultry, fish, Mexican dishes, soups, stews, eggs, cheese dishes, vegetables, spreads, French dressing, snacks.

Cinnamon: pork, chicken, lamb, soups, fruit, fruit salads, salad dressings, breads, pies, cakes, cookies, beverages, snacks.

Cloves: pork (especially ham), lamb, vegetables, relishes, pies, cakes, cookies, beverages, snacks.

Coriander: poultry, pork, curries, soups, stews, stuffings, fruit salads.

Cumin: Mexican dishes, cheese dishes, soups, stews, vegetable dips, sauces, salad dressings, snacks.

Curry powder: meats, fish, poultry, vegetables, soups, dips, cheese spreads, salads, dressings, chutneys, relishes.

Dill (weed and seed): meats, poultry, fish, seafood, stews, eggs, vegetables, salads, dressings, breads, sauces.

Fennel: meats, poultry, fish, seafood, soups, stews, vegetables, salads, dressings, pickles.

Garlic (clove, powder and salt): meats, poultry, casseroles, soups, stews, vegetables, dressings, sauces, marinades, pickles.

Ginger: Oriental dishes, meats, poultry, vegetables, cakes, cookies, pies, pickles.

Marjoram: meats, poultry, poultry stuffing, soups, stews, eggs, salads, sauces.

Mint: lamb, fish, poultry, vegetables, salads, fruit, sauces, marinades, desserts, beverages.

Mustard (dry and seed): corned beef, eggs, sauerkraut, macaroni salads, dressings, marinades, sauces, dips, pickles.

Nutmeg: meatloaves, meatballs, chicken, quiches, fruit, eggnog, cookies, cakes, pies.

Onion (flakes and minced): used interchangeably; often the same product; canned tuna or salmon, soups, salads, ground beef, lamb, oil-vinegar salad dressings.

Onion (powder and salt): chicken, beef, pork, stews, vegetables, soups, sauces.

Oregano: meats, poultry, fish, seafood, soups, stews, casseroles, eggs, vegetables, salads, breads.

Paprika: meats, fish, soups, stews, eggs, potatoes, sauces, cottage cheese.

Pepper (ground and freshly ground): meats, fish, poultry, eggs, salads, vegetables, marinades, pasta.

Poppy seed: pasta, breads, desserts.

Poultry seasoning: a pre-mixed combination of marjoram, savory, thyme and black pepper; used in poultry stuffing and other bread stuffings.

Red pepper (crushed and flakes): Mexican and Cajun dishes, eggs, dips, spreads, cream soups, French dressing.

Rosemary: meats, poultry, fish, casseroles, eggs, soups, stews, vegetables, salads, breads.

Saffron: the most expensive spice in the world; chicken, fish, seafood, rice, breads, cakes.

Sage: meats, poultry, soups, stews, casseroles, eggs, stuffings, vegetables, sauces.

Sesame seed: poultry, fish, vegetables, breads, cookies, salads, pasta.

Tarragon: meats, poultry, casseroles, fish, seafood, soups, stews, eggs, cheese dishes, vegetables, salads, dressings, sauces.

Thyme: meats, poultry, meatloaves, meatballs, fish, seafood, eggs, soups, stews, casseroles, vegetables, salads, breads, sauces, stuffings.

Turmeric: can be used in place of saffron; poultry, fish, eggs, soups, salad dressings, sauces, relishes, pickles.

▶ Because vinegar is highly volatile, its flavor dissipates with heat and air. To retain its pungent flavor, add vinegar to a cooked dish only after removing the dish from the heat. If a less pungent flavor is desired, add the vinegar while the dish is cooking and allow vinegar to boil off slightly.

▶ Types of Vinegar:

• **Balsamic vinegar** comes from Italy. Sweet white grape juice is placed in wooden barrels and fermented for at least 10 years and up to 70 years. The final product is dark, rich and sweet. It's great to add to sauces almost anytime.

• **Cider vinegar** is made from apple cider (apple cider vinegar). This golden brown vinegar is one of the most pungent. Use it to pickle vegetables or splash it in a hearty soup.

• **Distilled white vinegar** is colorless and is made from grain alcohol. It is the common vinegar used for household cooking. If it has an acidity of 5% or higher then it can also be used for preserving.

• **Malt vinegar** is caramel-colored and made from malted barley. It has a sharp, jarring flavor. Malt vinegar is a popular condiment for fish and chips in the British Isles.

• **Rice vinegar** is a Japanese vinegar made from sake. China and Thailand also have their versions, which are usually heavier and darker. Use rice vinegar to pickle vegetables or season rice. It may also be used as a dipping sauce for egg rolls.

• **Wine vinegar**, like wine, is available in red, white, sparkling, sherry and rosé. By law it must be 6 to 7% acidic. Wine vinegar can enhance a salad, perk up a main dish or even flavor berries.

▶ Cooking with Wine:

• Whether quickly making a deglazing sauce or simmering a dish over a long period, allow enough cooking time after adding wine for the alcohol to evaporate. Boiling a sauce rapidly in a shallow pan for 1 to 2 minutes will cook off the alcohol. Slow simmering in a deeper pan may take 15 minutes or more.

• Avoid adding wine to a sauce just before serving, or the dish may taste unpleasantly alcoholic.

• Boiling wine concentrates its flavors, acidity and sweetness. Be careful not to use too much or the finished dish may be excessively sweet or sour or taste too strongly of wine.

• Wine doesn't belong in every dish. More than one wine-based sauce in a meal can be monotonous. Use wine only when it has something to contribute to the finished dish.

My valuable tips:

Cooking Tips

General

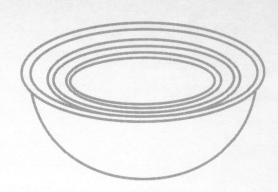

▶ To clarify butter, put into heavy saucepan over low heat just to melt. Skim off foam that forms on top. Slowly pour the clear butter into another container, leaving the milk solids in the pan. Discard. Clarified butter can be used for frying, sauteing or dipping lobster into and will not burn as easily as unclarified butter.

▶ To plump up raisins and dried fruit, cover with water and bring to a boil. Remove from heat. Let stand for 1 minute before draining. This method works for dried mushrooms too.

▶ To toast nuts (pecans, walnuts, almonds, or other), place in shallow pan. Bake in 350°F (175°C) oven for about 5 to 10 minutes, stirring often, until desired doneness. This works well for coconut too.

▶ If you have difficulty chopping parsley, hold briefly under hot running water and then squeeze-dry with paper towel. Chopping will be noticeably better. Or use your kitchen scissors to snip off just what you need in nice tiny bits.

▶ To tell if the inside of something you are heating up is hot, put the blade of a knife down into the center and hold for 10 seconds. Remove and hold the tip between your fingers for 5 seconds. If it feels very warm or hot, then your food is heated enough.

▶ To quickly thaw 1½ lbs. (680 g) ground beef, remove any wrapping and place in small bowl in microwave. Cover bowl with waxed paper. Microwave for 10 minutes on defrost (30%). Let sit in microwave for another 10 minutes. The meat should be thawed but not cooked and so can be used to make hamburgers or meatballs for a quick supper.

▶ The golden rule for the microwave oven - You can always add time but you can never take it away! Don't overheat food. It will toughen and dry out as it cools.

▶ To melt chocolate in the microwave, place in a small, deep microwave-safe bowl. Microwave on medium (50%) for 30 second intervals, stirring between each interval. The chocolate will keep its shape even when melted, so stirring is important. Reduce time to 10 seconds if you think chocolate is close to being melted. Then let it sit for about 30 seconds to complete the melting process.

▶ Always heat your frying pan before adding butter or cooking oil. Then add the oil and let it heat quickly. Add your meat or vegetables once the oil is hot. You won't have a problem with sticking.

▶ The best oil for deep-frying is lard or solid vegetable shortening, melted. Both are clear with a high smoke point (that means its ability to withstand high temperature without burning).

▶ Oil can be used 3 or 4 times before it has to be discarded. Oil will last longer if food particles are skimmed off after each batch of food has been fried. To store, add 2 tbsp. (30 mL) cornstarch. Stir. Cool. Strain through cheesecloth and keep in the refrigerator for up to 3 months.

▶ Hot liquids (such as oil or soup) can burn the careless cook or innocent onlooker. Turn the pot handle away from you, toward the counter so that it cannot be accidentally bumped.

Cooking Tips

Meats & Poultry

▶ Thaw meat and poultry in the refrigerator, giving yourself lots of time. Some cuts may take up to 2 or 3 days to thaw properly, depending on weight and bulk.

▶ A fork should never be stuck into a steak or pork chop that is being fried or grilled. It lets the juices out and dries out the meat.

▶ If sausages are boiled for about 8 minutes before being fried, they will shrink less and not break at all.

▶ If you pierce sausages with a fork or the tip of a knife as they are frying, you will release a lot of the fat. But remember, this will cause the sausages to shrink and to be a bit drier and more solid in texture.

▶ If meat is cooked at a lower temperature for a longer time there is less shrinkage.

▶ Prolonged boiling toughens meat. After the liquid has been added, bring it just to a boil. Then regulate the heat so that the liquid simmers gently for the rest of the cooking time.

▶ When you want to serve meatloaf but there is not enough time to cook it, divide it among muffin cups to cook in half the time.

▶ A sure way to eliminate excess fat when cooking meatloaf is to shape it and place on a rack set on a baking sheet with sides or in a roaster.

▶ Never crowd your pan when browning stew meat as it will steam instead of brown. Do it in scant single layer batches to get that nice even browning.

▶ Preheat your frying pan or saucepan before adding meat. Meat needs to stick slightly to the pan as it browns so that its juices can caramelize. Do not stir it too often as this inhibits the caramelizing process.

▶ An easy way to make sure all your meatballs come out the same size is to pat the meat mixture into a 1 inch (2.5 cm) thick square on waxed paper. Cut the square into 1 inch (2.5 cm) cubes. Dip your hands into water and gently roll the cubes into balls.

▶ Always marinate meat and poultry in the refrigerator, not on the counter.

▶ For quick cleanup marinate meat and poultry in a sealable plastic bag and just throw the bag away when finished.

▶ For a quick grilling trick, combine fresh meat or poultry (intended for the barbecue) in a freezer bag along with your favorite marinade. It will be ready to grill as soon as it has thawed.

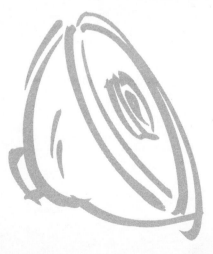

▶ Thoroughly clean cutting board or plate with hot soapy water immediately after raw chicken, or any raw meat or fish, has been on it.

▶ Cook chicken thoroughly. Chicken or turkeys with bones should register 190°F (90°C) on a meat thermometer. Boneless parts should be cooked to an internal temperature of 170°F (75°C).

▶ After coating chicken with a flour or crumb base, chill for 1 hour. The coating will adhere better during cooking.

▶ About 1 lb. (454 g) raw boneless chicken will yield 2 cups (500 mL) chopped cooked chicken.

▶ To speed up the thawing process of a whole turkey or chicken, leave it in its wrapping. Immerse in a bowl of cold water and place in the refrigerator. Change the water regularly. Never thaw at room temperature.

▶ Always stuff an uncooked turkey or chicken just before cooking.

▶ Always remove stuffing immediately after cooking chicken or turkey.

▶ An easy way to truss your bird is to use dental floss as it doesn't burn and is very strong.

Cooking Tips

Pasta & Rice

▶ To make perfect pasta every time, always put pasta into rapidly boiling water. Use at least 1 quart (1 L) water for every 4 oz. (113 g) uncooked pasta.

▶ Test pasta for doneness according to package directions. Pasta should be tender but still firm (al dente) when you bite into it.

▶ Fresh pasta cooks much faster than dried pasta. Fresh pasta only takes 2 to 3 minutes, so check it frequently.

▶ Use a flat, metal skimmer or a flat, slotted spoon to lift cooked, filled pasta such as ravioli or tortellini out of the water. Immediately toss in oil or sauce to prevent sticking.

▶ Use a sealable plastic bag with 1 corner cut off, to pipe filling inside manicotti shells. It's quick and cleanup is easy.

▶ If you have a small amount of several different pastas of similar size, cook them together and use in soups, salads or casseroles.

▶ Choose whole wheat pasta for high-fiber, healthy pasta dishes. If the whole wheat pasta is too heavy on its own, mix equal amount with regular pasta.

▶ Types of Rice:

• Arborio rice is a medium grain rice and absorbs more liquid than other types of rice. Risotto, a popular Italian dish, is made with this rice.

• **Basmati rice** is slightly longer than regular white rice. It is very fragrant and is not as starchy as other rice so stays separated.

• **Glutinous rice**, used mainly in Chinese cooking (especially sushi), is a round short grain rice with a sticky texture.

• **Long grain rice** may be brown or white, regular or converted. Converted rice is not as starchy and has had the nutrients added back in.

• To cook **brown rice**, bring 2 cups (500 mL) lightly salted water to a boil for every 1 cup (250 mL) brown rice. Stir once with fork. Cover. Reduce heat to low. Cook for 35 to 45 minutes. Remove from heat and let stand for 5 minutes. Fluff with fork.

• To cook **white rice**, bring 1½ cups (375 mL) lightly salted water to a boil for every 1 cup (250 mL) white rice. Stir once with fork. Cover. Reduce heat to low. Cook for 15 to 18 minutes. Remove from heat and let stand for 5 minutes. Fluff with fork.

• **Pearl rice** is a short grain polished white rice. It is soft and starchy when cooked and used mainly in rice pudding.

• **Wild rice** is the seed of a wild, aquatic grass. It is best used in combination with white or brown rice. Wild rice is often used in stuffing for Cornish hens.

• To cook **wild rice**, bring 2½ cups (625 mL) lightly salted water to a boil for every 1 cup (250 mL) wild rice. Stir once with fork. Cover. Reduce heat to low. Cook for 45 to 50 minutes. Remove from heat and let stand for 5 minutes. Fluff with fork.

Cooking Tips

Vegetables

Artichokes

▶ To prepare artichokes, soak them in salted water for 30 minutes to eliminate any insects. Cut stem from the base to make a flat bottom. Cut about 1 inch (2.5 cm) off the top of the artichoke. Trim the spiky tops off the outer leaves with kitchen scissors. Immediately rub all cut surfaces with lemon juice or vinegar to prevent blackening. Pry the leaves open and scoop the inedible fuzzy choke from the center. To use just the heart, trim away all the leaves, then pare the heart out with a small knife.

▶ Cook artichokes, stem end down, in a large amount of boiling salted water. Cover. Cook for 20 to 30 minutes until a leaf pulls out easily. Or place in steamer basket and steam, covered, for 20 to 25 minutes. Invert to drain. To microwave, place artichokes and about 2 tbsp. (30 mL) water in a microwave-safe casserole. Do not salt. Microwave, covered, on high (100%), rearranging once, for 7 to 9 minutes until a leaf pulls out easily.

▶ Thoroughly cook artichokes to kill the natural enzymes that will cause the flesh to turn black even before cutting.

▶ To eat an artichoke, pull off leaves one at a time. Hold leaf by the top and dip base into melted butter (or margarine) or sauce. Scrape the fleshy part off of the base with your teeth. Once most of the leaves have been removed, discard the fuzzy center or "choke." Eat the remaining base with a knife and fork.

Asparagus

▶ To cut asparagus, hold bottom of spear with one hand and just under the tip with the other hand. Bend the stalk until it snaps and breaks at the point where toughness stops.

▶ Cook asparagus by laying spears in boiling salted water in wide saucepan. Cook, covered, for 3 to 6 minutes. Or place in steamer basket and steam, covered, for the same amount of time. To microwave, lay in shallow casserole or baking dish, with tips overlapping in the center. Add only enough water to half cover. Do not salt. Cover dish with lid or lay a piece of waxed paper over top. Microwave on high (100%) for 7 to 9 minutes.

Bell Peppers

▶ Come in 4 colors - green, red, yellow and orange. Each color has a different flavor but all are considered mild. Green is the mildest, with red being the sweetest. They can be used in a variety of ways: stir-fries, stuffed, in salads or eaten raw.

▶ Can be finely diced and cooked in scrambled eggs, chopped and thrown into a salad, or slivered and used in a stir-fry. Roasting over a hot burner or grill is popular and makes a tasty sauce for meat or pasta.

▶ Are generally expensive, particularly the yellow and orange ones. Be sure to buy them only when you have a specific recipe in mind. If you only need a portion of one, cut it and only seed the portion needed. Place the unused portion in a sealable plastic bag and place in vegetable drawer in refrigerator. Use as quickly as possible.

Broccoli ▶ To prepare broccoli, trim stalks and remove leaves. Peel stalks. Cut stems into smaller pieces and separate florets.

▶ Cook broccoli, covered, in a small amount of boiling salted water for 8 to 12 minutes. Or place in steamer basket and steam, covered, for 8 to 12 minutes. To microwave, place in microwave-safe casserole with florets overlapping in center. Add about 2 tbsp. (30 mL) water. Do not salt. Cover. Microwave on high (100%) for 4 to 7 minutes.

Cabbage ▶ Cook cabbage, uncovered, in a small amount of boiling water for 2 minutes. This will allow the release of the sulphur compounds into the air and keep the pungent smell down. Cover. Cook wedges for an additional 6 to 8 minutes and pieces for an additional 3 to 5 minutes. To microwave, place cabbage and about 2 tbsp. (30 mL) water in a microwave-safe casserole. Do not salt. Cover. Microwave wedges on high (100%) for 9 to 11 minutes or pieces for 4 to 6 minutes.

▶ Chinese cabbage cooks in less time than more common cabbage varieties but can be prepared in the same ways: steamed, boiled, microwaved, stuffed or stir-fried. The last method is the most popular.

▶ When making coleslaw or sauerkraut it's helpful to know a 2 lb. (900 g) head of cabbage yields about 10 cups (2.5 L) shredded cabbage.

Carrots ▶ Cook carrots, covered, in a small amount of boiling salted water for 7 to 9 minutes. Or place in steamer basket and steam, covered, for 8 to 10 minutes. To microwave, place carrots and about 2 tbsp. (30 mL) water in a microwave-safe casserole. Do not salt. Microwave, covered, on high (100%), stirring once, for 4 to 6 minutes.

Cauliflower ▶ Cook a head of cauliflower, covered, in a small amount of boiling salted water for 10 to 15 minutes. Cook florets for 8 to 10 minutes. Or place florets in steamer basket and steam for 8 to 12 minutes. Place a head of cauliflower and about 2 tbsp. (30 mL) water in a microwave-safe casserole. Do not salt. Cover. Microwave on high (100%), stirring once, for 9 to 11 minutes (7 to 10 minutes for florets).

▶ To keep cauliflower white, add 1 to 2 tsp. (5 to 10 mL) white vinegar to the boiling water.

Corn ▶ When cooking corn, do not add salt to the water as salt toughens corn. Instead, add 1 tsp. (5 mL) sugar. Try not to overcook as it only takes a few minutes (between 4 - 7 minutes), depending on the size.

Eggplant ▶ Most recipes call for slicing and salting eggplant first. This draws the excess moisture out and reduces a lot of the bitterness that is associated with eggplant.

▶ Eggplant can be cooked in a variety of ways: baked, broiled or grilled. Be sure to pierce whole eggplant with a fork to allow steam to escape. To microwave whole, microwave on high (100%) for 6 to 8 minutes. Microwave cubed salted eggplant in about 2 tbsp. (30 mL) water, covered, on high (100%) for 3 to 4 minutes.

Hot Peppers ▶ Contain capsaicin that gives these peppers their heat. Capsaicin is found only in the seeds and ribs of the peppers. You can easily "lower the heat" of a recipe that calls for whole hot peppers by cutting them in half and removing the seeds and ribs.

▶ When handling hot peppers, such as jalapeño, it is best to wear thin rubber gloves. The heat is in the seeds and ribs so be particularly careful when handling these parts. Avoid touching your eyes. Rinse hands well.

Onions ▶ Place onion under cold running water when cutting. It will keep your eyes from watering and also cut down on the onion smell.

▶ Rub a few drops of vinegar on your hands before handling or cutting onions. Your hands will end up odor-free.

▶ Always keep at least 1 onion in the refrigerator. A cold onion, when being cut, doesn't emit the vapors that cause your eyes to water.

Parsnips ▶ Parsnips are almost always eaten cooked as they tend to be quite fibrous. Be careful not to overcook them. Either scrub or peel the parsnips, depending on how you plan to prepare them.

Pea Pods ▶ Cook fresh snow (Chinese) pea pods in a small amount of boiling salted water in a covered saucepan for 2 to 4 minutes or until tender-crisp. Or steam for 2 to 4 minutes. To microwave, place pea pods and 2 tbsp. (30 mL) water in a microwave-safe casserole. Microwave on high (100%) for 3 to 5 minutes or until tender-crisp.

Peas ▶ Cook fresh peas, covered, in a small amount of boiling salted water for 7 to 9 minutes. Or place in steamer basket, covered, for 10 to 12 minutes. To microwave, place peas and about 2 tbsp. (30 mL) water in microwave-safe casserole. Do not salt. Cover. Microwave on high (100%), stirring once, for 6 to 8 minutes.

Spinach ▶ Fresh cooked spinach and thawed frozen spinach can be used interchangeably in recipes.

▶ Most cooked spinach (or thawed frozen spinach) needs to be squeeze-dried before adding to recipe. Take small amount in one hand and squeeze. Let juice run into sink. Squeeze several times for each handful.

▶ Cook spinach, covered, in a small amount of boiling salted water for 3 to 5 minutes. Begin timing when steam forms. Or place in steamer basket and steam, covered, for 3 to 5 minutes. To microwave, place spinach and about 2 tbsp. (30 mL) water in a microwave-safe casserole. Do not salt. Cover. Microwave on high (100%), stirring once, for 4 to 6 minutes.

Squash ▶ There are a number of different squashes that are popular: acorn, butternut, hubbard and spaghetti.

▶ It is best to bake squash in the oven rather than boiling it in water. Leave the squash in its shell; cut into desired pieces. Brush cut sides with olive oil. Place, cut side down, in baking pan. Cover with lid or foil. Bake in 375°F (190°C) oven for 45 to 60 minutes until soft when pierced with a fork. Scoop out seeds. Serve with or without the shell.

Tomatoes ▶ Almost everyone slices a tomato crosswise. Cut it from top to bottom instead. More juice is retained and you will have a different "look."

▶ When cooking with tomatoes, tomato sauce or tomato paste, add some granulated sugar. Even ½ tsp. (2 mL) makes quite a difference in cutting the acidity.

My valuable tips:

_____

_____

_____

_____

_____

_____

_____

_____

Cooking
Tips

Shortcuts

Baby Food ▶ Instead of buying baby food, purchase frozen vegetables and purée them in your food processor. Spoon into ice cube trays and freeze. Empty into freezer bags for easy storage and use.

Bacon ▶ When a recipe calls for chopped bacon, use kitchen scissors. Or cut the bacon when partially frozen.

Barbecue ▶ Spray your cold barbecue grill with vegetable or canola oil before barbecuing to make cleanup easier.

Beaters ▶ Lightly spray beaters with no-stick cooking spray before mixing cake and cookie batters to prevent clumping.

Bread ▶ To freshen dried bread, wrap in damp tea towel, place in plastic bag, and refrigerate for 24 hours. Remove tea towel and heat bread in oven for a few minutes.

▶ For quick and easy garlic bread sticks, split a hot dog bun down the middle and cut each half lengthwise. Butter and sprinkle with garlic powder or garlic salt. Place under broiler until toasted.

▶ 1 slice of bread will make about ¾ cup (175 mL) fresh bread crumbs or about ¼ cup (60 mL) fine dry bread crumbs.

Cakes ▶ Whenever you make a homemade cake, get a head start by measuring the dry ingredients into sealable plastic bags. Label the bag with the recipe name and instructions. It's more economical and really quick to whip up a cake when company comes.

Chocolate ▶ When melting chocolate chips for decorating, place them in a plastic bag and put into the microwave or into a pan of hot water. Knead the bag to smooth the chocolate, then cut 1 small hole in corner of the bag to pipe out the chocolate.

Cookies ▶ Children can easily prepare cutout cookies using this method. Roll out dough on lightly greased cookie sheet. Cut out as many cookies as possible with a bit of space between them, then peel away the dough scrapes.

▶ When sprinkling sugar on cookies, use a salt shaker or empty spice bottle.

Cupcakes ▶ When you're ready to frost the cupcakes you've made to pack in lunches, cut them in half, frost the centers and put back together. This way, the frosting won't stick to the sandwich bags.

Dressing

▶ For a quick dressing, shake balsamic vinegar and olive oil together. The portions are up to you, but equal amounts or slightly more vinegar works best. There's no need to measure - just use your nose and you will know if it's right.

▶ For a quick bread dip, pour olive oil onto a small plate. Gently pour some balsamic vinegar into the oil. Do not mix. Serve with chunks of bread.

▶ Use salad dressing for ready-made marinades or seasoned oil for cooking meats and poultry.

▶ When making mayonnaise, add oil to the egg yolks slowly in a thin stream; otherwise, the mayonnaise separates.

▶ Vinaigrettes will separate upon standing. To re-emulsify a dressing simply shake or whisk it.

Garlic Cloves

▶ To keep garlic cloves from sprouting, softening and drying out, keep them in a container in the freezer. Peel and chop before thawing.

▶ To easily pop the skin off a garlic clove, place in microwave. Heat on high (100%) for 30 seconds.

Gravy

▶ To make smooth gravy, mix flour and water in a jar, shake well until smooth then pour into the hot liquid to thicken.

▶ If you find your gravy has gone lumpy run it through the blender. This works like a charm.

▶ If the gravy is just about gone but the roast isn't, don't use expensive gravy mixes. Instead, use beef or chicken bouillon powder to stretch beef, chicken and turkey gravy. Add 1 to 2 tsp. (5 to 10 mL) bouillon powder to a glass of water. Add all-purpose flour or cornstarch. Mix with a fork and add the leftover gravy. Reheat to thicken.

Honey ▶ If your honey has crystallized, remove lid and place container in a boiling pot of water, or place open container in the microwave and microwave on high (100%) for 15 second intervals. Stir often until crystals have dissolved.

Ice Cream ▶ Before guests arrive for a birthday party scoop ice cream balls onto cookie sheet lined with waxed paper and refreeze. You won't have to fuss later when serving cake.

Ice Cubes ▶ Make a batch of ice cubes using lemonade or iced tea. Your drink won't be watered down.

Jellied Salad ▶ Removing jellied salads from their molds doesn't have to be tricky. Quickly dip the mold into very warm water for about 10 seconds. Gently pull the salad away from the edges of the mold with your fingertips. Invert the plate over the mold then, holding them together, invert them back. Shake the mold gently back and forth (rather than up and down) until you feel the salad loosen. Or hold the plate and mold at an angle and gently shake. Carefully lift the mold off. If salad doesn't unmold, repeat these steps. Using a hot cloth might work better on metal molds to prevent excessive softening on outer edge of salad (especially a salad containing whipped cream, mayonnaise or sour cream).

▶ Brush wet hand over plate before placing over mold. It will be easier to move the unmolded salad to center it.

Ketchup ▶ Having trouble getting the ketchup to pour out of the bottle? Insert a drinking straw, push it to the bottom of the bottle and then remove it. Enough air will be admitted to start an even flow.

Lettuce ▶ When washing freshly picked greens, soak them in cold water with a little vinegar for 10 minutes to remove any tiny insects.

Marinating ▶ When marinating vegetables, put them into a container with a tight-fitting lid. No stirring needed. Just turn the jar or bowl upside down every few minutes for even marinating.

▶ If you don't have a large enough container to immerse meat or fish in a marinade, use a sealable plastic bag. It's easy to jostle the marinade around and to turn the bag over every so often.

Meatballs ▶ When making meatballs for spaghetti, first boil them in water until they rise to the top of the pan. Drain and add them to the sauce to finish cooking. This eliminates the mess of frying and cuts some fat from the meat.

Muffins: ▶ To reheat muffins, wrap them loosely in foil, then heat in a 450°F (230°C) oven for about 5 minutes. Or heat in the microwave on high (100%) for 10 seconds

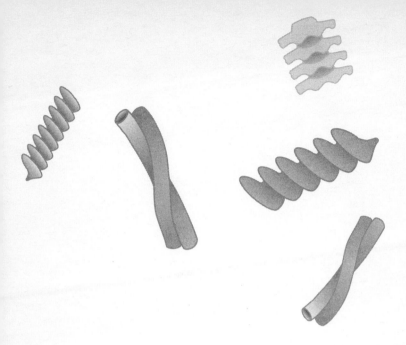

Nuts ▶ To crush nuts easily and to prevent them from going all over your kitchen, put them into a sealable plastic bag and roll with a rolling pin. This also works with cookies for cookie crumbs.

▶ Before chopping nuts in the food processor, dust them with all-purpose flour so they don't stick to the blades.

Pancakes ▶ Mix prepared pancake batter in a pitcher for a no-fuss method of making pancakes. They are easy to pour with no drippy edges and the extra batter can be refrigerated with the lid on.

Pasta ▶ Rinse leftover pasta with cold water before putting into the refrigerator so it won't stick together.

Pastry Brush ▶ Dampen your pastry brush before dipping it into oil. This prevents it from soaking up the oil.

▶ A small 2 inch (5 cm) good quality paintbrush will last longer and stay more pliable than a pastry brush.

Pickling Spice ▶ When you don't have any cheesecloth on hand to make a bag for pickling spices, use a coffee filter or clean nylon stocking.

Pies ▶ If the juice from your pies runs over in the oven, shake some salt on the spill. This causes the juice to burn to a crisp so it can be removed.

Popcorn ▶ Store popcorn in the freezer. It will pop without leaving so many unpopped kernels.

Potatoes ▶ If your potatoes sprout before you can use them, peel, slice and boil them until partially cooked. Remove from water and freeze in small batches. When you want mashed potato put the frozen potatoes into boiling water to finish cooking.

▶ To save time when making your favorite potato salad, peel and dice potatoes to desired size before cooking. They will cook much faster and won't require further cutting. Be careful not to cook too long.

▶ When time is short and you want baked potatoes, boil them, unpeeled, for about 10 minutes before baking them in a 400°F (205°C) oven.

Poultry ▶ When stuffing a large turkey, line the cavity with cheesecloth and then place stuffing inside. After the turkey is cooked, the stuffing is easy to get out and nothing is left clinging to the bones.

▶ There's no need to sew up a turkey or chicken after stuffing it. Just fit a heel of bread over the opening.

▶ To make chicken easier to dice or slice, place it in the freezer for about 30 minutes or until it is just beginning to freeze. Or if using from frozen state, only partially thaw. Then cut according to recipe instructions. This also works for other cuts of meat.

Sauces ▶ To make fast pasta sauce, mix a can of crushed tomatoes and an envelope of Italian dressing mix.

▶ If your Hollandaise or Béarnaise sauce separates, whisk in 1 tbsp. (15 mL) cold water with 1 tbsp. (15 mL) of the separated sauce until the mixture is smooth. Gradually whisk in the remaining separated sauce. Or whisk 1 egg yolk with 1 tbsp. (15 mL) water in saucepan until thickened. Slowly whisk in separated sauce.

Sifting ▶ Sift large quantities, such as flour mixtures, onto a sheet of waxed paper. Carefully lift the paper and funnel the mixture into the bowl. Use the paper to hold the spatula after you've scraped the bowl. You will have fewer dishes to wash and your counter will stay clean.

Soup ▶ If your homemade soup is too salty, drop a raw potato into the pot and remove just before serving.

▶ When making big batches of soup, pour soup into large, medium or small bowls and freeze. Once frozen, the soup can be popped out of the bowls and stored in large sealable freezer bags. This also makes a nice gift for an ill friend or someone living alone.

▶ The best method for making soup, when you have time, is to place it in the refrigerator until the fat hardens on top. Then just lift or skim it off.

▶ Instant potato flakes make a quick, low-fat soup thickener. Stir in 1 tbsp. (15 mL) at a time, cook for 1 minute and then add more as necessary.

▶ A big pot with a strainer insert is handy for making soup stock. Put the meat bones and vegetables into the strainer, fill the pot with water and cook. When it's time to strain the broth, just lift out and no bones will remain in the broth.

▶ Pour cooled broth from meat or poultry into a glass jar with a secure lid. Refrigerate upside down. The fat will harden and remain in the jar when you pour out the liquid to use in recipes.

Spices ▶ If your spice cupboard is a mess, try putting your spices into a deep drawer or a pullout bottom shelf. Label the tops of the containers and arrange them in alphabetical order.

Spicy Foods ▶ After eating something spicy, try a dairy product such as milk, yogurt or sour cream. Water only spreads the capsaicin (the compound that makes the peppers hot) around but doesn't cure the burn.

Squeeze Bottles ▶ Use clean plastic squeeze bottles to dispense the right amount of sour cream or mayonnaise on tacos, hamburgers, etc. Make sure you copy the expiry date from the original container on the squeeze bottle.

Tomatoes ▶ To easily pop the skin off a tomato, place in microwave. Heat on high (100%) for 40 to 60 seconds depending on size of tomato.

Unexpected Company ▶ When company shows up unexpectedly, stretch a thick stew by adding a few more vegetables or a can of tomatoes to it and serving over rice, noodles or mashed potato.

▶ If you're having soup for lunch when unexpected company arrives, quickly cook some pasta and add to soup. This is a great meal stretcher. You can also add a can of tomatoes depending on the flavor of soup.

Whipped Cream ▶ Spoon dabs of leftover whipped cream onto waxed paper and place in the freezer. When they are frozen, place in a sealable plastic bag and keep in the freezer to use for dessert toppings. They thaw in 10 to 15 minutes.

▶ When whipping cream, use icing (confectioner's) sugar as it will keep the whipped cream fluffy longer than if you use granulated sugar.

Wooden Picks ▶ Store wooden picks in an empty spice bottle with a shake top. Just shake one out through the holes. No fumbling in the box.

Yeast Dough ▶ If you're in a hurry to get yeast dough to rise, bring a pot of water to a boil. Turn the heat to low. Place a rack over the top, set the bowl of dough on the rack and cover with a tea towel.

My valuable tips:

_____

_____

_____

_____

_____

_____

_____

Cooking Tips

Substitutions

Baking Powder ▶ If you don't have baking powder, substitute ½ tsp. (2 mL) cream of tartar and ¼ tsp. (1 mL) baking soda for 1 tsp. (5 mL) baking powder.

Beef Broth ▶ If you don't have a can of condensed beef broth, you can substitute 2 tsp. (10 mL) beef bouillon powder and 1¼ cups (300 mL) boiling water.

Bread Pudding ▶ For really great tasting bread pudding, substitute leftover sweet buns for bread slices.

Brown Sugar ▶ Out of brown sugar? For every ½ cup (125 mL) needed, mix ½ cup (125 mL) granulated sugar, ½ tsp. (2 mL) each maple flavoring and fancy molasses. This is a little more moist than brown sugar, but tastes the same.

Chocolate Baking Sqares ▶ If you don't have any chocolate baking squares substitute 3 tbsp. (50 mL) cocoa plus 1 tbsp. (15 mL) shortening for each square. It's just as good and a lot less expensive.

Eggs ▶ If you are on a cholesterol-restricted diet, replace whole eggs with egg whites whenever you can. The egg whites contain no cholesterol or fat. You can substitute 2 egg whites for 1 whole egg in many recipes. You'll need to do a little experimenting with recipes, especially those for baked goods.

Flour ▶ If you don't have cake flour, measure the required amount of all-purpose flour, and take out 1 tbsp. (15 mL) from each cup, replacing with 1 tbsp. (15 mL) cornstarch. Or just use $\frac{7}{8}$ cup (220 mL) all-purpose flour for every 1 cup (250 mL) cake flour.

▶ To make self-rising flour, mix 2½ tsp. (12 mL) baking powder and 1 cup (250 mL) all-purpose flour. Use in the same quantities as self-rising flour.

Garlic Clove ▶ 1 medium clove of garlic is equal to ¼ tsp. (1 mL) garlic powder.

Mashing Potatoes ▶ When mashing potatoes, use cream cheese, sour cream or salad dressing (or mayonnaise) instead of milk.

▶ Use skim milk powder in mashed potatoes instead of milk. They will be fluffier and you won't have to drain them so well; the powder will absorb excess water. But if you find they are too dry, add a bit of hot water until desired texture.

Milk ▶ For 1 cup (250 mL) buttermilk, substitute ¼ cup (60 mL) whole milk plus ¾ cup (175 mL) plain yogurt. Or add ½ tsp. (2 mL) baking powder to 1 cup (250 mL) milk. Or you can use sour milk.

▶ If you run out of milk, substitute ½ cup (125 mL) evaporated milk and ½ cup (125 mL) water. Or reconstitute ⅓ cup (75 mL) skim milk powder in 1 cup (250 mL) water.

▶ If you don't have sour milk and need some for a recipe, place 1 tbsp. (15 mL) white vinegar in a measuring cup. Fill with milk to 1 cup (250 mL). If milk is a touch warm all the better. Let stand for 5 minutes.

Onions ▶ Just used your last onion? You can substitute 1 tbsp. (15 mL) onion flakes or 1 tsp. (5 mL) onion powder for ¼ cup (60 mL) chopped onion.

Pasta ▶ 4 cups (1 L) uncooked macaroni is equal to 1 lb. (454 g).

Salt/Pepper ▶ Since most recipes call for both salt and pepper, keep a shaker filled with a mixture of 3 parts salt to 1 part pepper - it eliminates the need for measuring.

Sour Cream ▶ Process creamed cottage cheese in blender until smooth. You can use it in dips, instead of sour cream.

Wine ▶ If a recipe calls for wine and you would prefer to avoid alcohol (or don't want to open a bottle for only a small amount):

• for white wine, substitute white grape juice or apple juice.

• for red wine, substitute red wine vinegar to which you have added granulated sugar.

Wooden Picks ▶ If you run out of wooden picks or don't have a cake tester, use an uncooked spaghetti noodle.

Yogurt ▶ To add fresh fruit flavor to yogurt, buy plain yogurt, add any fresh fruit and process in blender.

My valuable tips:

_____

_____

_____

_____

_____

_____

_____

_____

_____

_____

_____

Measurements

Conventional And Metric Measures

Our measuring tools and the measurements given in cookbooks can be in either, or both, Conventional (Imperial) and Metric amounts. Here are some of the more common measurements in both forms:

Oven Temperatures

Fahrenheit (°F)	Celsius (°C)
175°	80°
200°	95°
225°	110°
250°	120°
275°	140°
300°	150°
325°	160°
350°	175°
375°	190°
400°	205°
425°	220°
450°	230°
475°	240°
500°	260°

Measuring Spoons

Conventional	Metric
1/8 teaspoon	0.5 mL
1/4 teaspoon	1 mL
1/2 teaspoon	2 mL
1 teaspoon	5 mL
1 1/2 teaspoon	7 mL
2 teaspoons	10 mL
1 tablespoon	15 mL
1 1/2 tablespoons	22 mL

Measuring Cups

Conventional	Metric
1/4 cup	60 mL
1/3 cup	75 mL
1/2 cup	125 mL
2/3 cup	150 mL
3/4 cup	175 mL
1 cup	250 mL
4 cups	1000 mL (1 L)

Weight Measures

Conventional	Metric
1 oz.	28 g
1 1/2 oz.	42 g
2 oz.	57 g
3 oz.	85 g
4 oz. (1/4 lb.)	113 g
5 oz.	150 g
6 oz.	170 g
7 oz.	200 g
8 oz. (1 lb.)	454 g
16 oz. (2 lbs.)	900 g

Pan Sizes

Conventional	Metric
8 x 8 inch	20 x 20 cm
9 x 9 inch	22 x 22 cm
9 x 13 inch	22 x 33 cm
10 X 15 inch	25 x 38 cm
11 x 17 inch	28 x 43 cm
8 x 4 x 3 inch loaf	20 x 10 x 7.5 cm
9 x 5 x 3 inch loaf	22 x 12.5 x 7.5cm
8 inch round	20 cm round
9 inch round	22 cm round

Index

Pastry brush - dampening before dipping
into oil, 49; substitute for, 49
Pea pods - to cook, 42
Pearl rice - description of, 36
Peas, to cook, 42
Peas, black-eyed (black-eyed beans) -
description of 16
Peas, split - as quick-cooking substitute, 16
Pecans - to toast, 30
Pepper (ground and freshly ground) - mixed with
salt, 57; uses of, 27
Peppers, bell - description of, 38; to buy, 38;
ways to use, 38
Peppers, hot - handling and preparation of, 41
Pickling spice - to make a bag for, 50
Pie shell - to bake unfilled, 12
Pies - double crust finish, 11; to clean
spills, 50; with meringue, 11
Pies, fruit - how much sugar, 11; spills in
oven, 11; thickeners for, 11; to clean spills, 50
PInch - description of, 25
Pinto beans - description of, 18
Plump - dried fruit, 30
Popcorn - storage of for better popping, 50
Poppy seed - uses of, 27
Potato salad - to save time, 50
Potatoes - additions to mashed, 56;
cooking time-savers, 50; if sprouting, 50
Poultry - marinating for quick cleanup, 33;
marinating for quick grilling, 33;
proper marinating, 33; to coat pieces, 34;
to determine yield amount, 34; to easily
cut boneless, 51; to safely prepare
and cook, 34; to speed up thawing of, 34;
to stuff, 51; to truss easily, 34
Poultry seasoning - uses of, 27
Pound cake - for best texture, 7
Preheating - before adding oil, 31; frying pan, 22;
oven, 10; when to preheat, 33
Pudding - bread pudding substitute, 55;
rice in, 36; to prevent burning of, 10

Q

Quick breads - baking, 13; greasing pans, 13;
to remove, 13; to restore freshness of, 45

R

Raisins - to plump, 30
Red bell pepper - ways to cook, 38
Red pepper (crushed and flakes) -
uses of, 27
Rice - descriptions and uses of:
arborio, 36
basmati, 36

brown, 36; to cook, 36
glutinous, 36
long grain, 36; to cook, 36
pearl, 36
white, 36; to cook, 36
wild, 36; to cook, 36
Rice vinegar - uses of, 28
Rosemary - uses of, 27

S

Saffron - uses of, 27
Sage - uses of, 27
Salad dressing (see Dressing)
Salt, pepper - shortcut for, 57
Sauces - adding wine, 29; deglazing, 29;
fast pasta, 51; if separates, 51
Sausages - to boil, 32; to pierce, 32
Self-rising flour - substitute for, 56
Sesame seed - uses of, 27
Sifting - easy cleanup, 52; large quantities, 52
Soup - adding spices to, 25; if too salty, 52;
stretching for unexpected company, 53;
to freeze for later use, 52; to skim the fat, 52;
to strain soup bones, 52; to thicken, 52
Sour cream - convenient storage of, 53;
substitute for, 58
Sour milk - substitute for, 57
Spices - to organize, 52
Spices & Herbs - description and uses of:
allspice, 25
basil, 25
bay leaf, 25
caraway seed, 25
cardamom, 25
celery (seed and salt), 25
chili powder, 25
cinnamon, 26
cloves, 26
coriander, 26
cumin, 26
curry powder, 25, 26
dill (weed and seed), 25, 26
fennel, 26
garlic (clove, powder
and salt), 26, 46, 56
ginger, 26
marjoram, 26
mint, 26
mustard (dry and seed), 26
nutmeg, 26
onion (flakes and minced), 25, 26, 57
onion (powder and salt), 27, 57
oregano, 27
paprika, 27

www.companyscoming.com
visit our web-site